Day Trading Psychology

Mastering the Mental Game for Consistent Profits.

CHINEDU BROWN

Copyright© 2024 Chinedu Brown

All rights reserved

To say thank you for purchasing this book, I offer you a free Video Course and more as a token of appreciation

Find the link to the Video Course at the end of this book.

Table of Contents

INTRODUCTION 4

   THE ROLE OF PSYCHOLOGY IN DAY TRADING 4
      The Mental Game of Day Trading 5
      Important Psychological Challenges in Day Trading 6
      Why Psychology Is Important for Consistent Profitability 9

CHAPTER ONE 14

   DEVELOPING EMOTIONAL DISCIPLINE 14
      Recognize Emotional Triggers 15
      Managing Fear and Greed in Trading 16
      Staying Emotionally Neutral 18
      Practical Techniques for Developing Emotional Discipline 20
      The Long-Term Advantages of Emotional Discipline 21

CHAPTER TWO 24

   DEVELOPING CONFIDENCE AND RESILIENCE 24
      The Importance of Confidence in Day Trading 25
      Staying Resilient Following Losses 27
      How to Develop Lasting Confidence and Resilience 28
      Importance of Bouncing Back 30
      Maintaining Balance Throughout Winning Streaks 32
      Building Long-term Confidence and Resilience 33

CHAPTER THREE 36

   MASTERING FOCUS AND CONCENTRATION 36
      The Advantages of Mental Clarity in Trading 37
      Techniques for Staying Mentally Sharp 38
      Avoiding Distractions in a Stressful Environment 41

CHAPTER FOUR 48

   IMPULSE CONTROL AND OVERTRADING 48

CHAPTER FIVE 60

   MANAGING ANXIETY AND TRADING PRESSURE 60
      Techniques to Stay Calm and Collected 64

Recognizing and Reducing Stress..*67*
Managing Emotions During Winning and Losing Streaks....................*68*

CHAPTER SIX..72

MANAGING EMOTIONS DURING WINNING AND LOSING STREAKS 72
Emotional Impact of Winning Streaks...*73*
Techniques to Stay Grounded...*80*

CHAPTER SEVEN 84

ESTABLISHING A GROWTH-ORIENTED ROUTINE..84
Importance of Routine in Day Trading *85*

CHAPTER EIGHT 96

JOURNALING FOR IMPROVEMENT. 96
Why Journaling Matters in Day Trading *97*
The Effects of Journaling on Emotional Awareness...........................*101*

CHAPTER NINE 108

SETTING REALISTIC PROFIT GOALS. 108
Why Do Realistic Goals Matter?..*109*
Recognizing and adjusting unrealistic expectations. *115*
Using Goal Setting to Build Confidence *116*
Setting Goals Beyond Just Profit..*117*

CONCLUSION..120

THE PATH TO UNDERSTANDING DAY TRADING PSYCHOLOGY....................120
Setting Realistic Expectations and Goals for Sustainable Growth. *127*

Introduction

The Role of Psychology in Day Trading

When most individuals think about day trading, they see sophisticated charts, market analysis, and the constant monitoring of financial data. While technical abilities are key, there is another aspect of day trading that is equally, if not more, important: the mental game. In fact, it is generally stated that psychology accounts for more than 80% of trading success, with strategy and analysis accounting for the remainder. Mastering the mental component of trading is critical to maintaining profitability and avoiding frequent errors. In this introduction, we'll look at why psychology is crucial in day trading and what mental hurdles traders commonly face.

The Mental Game of Day Trading

Day trading is a fast-paced and strenuous pursuit. Every day, traders enter a market with prices that can move dramatically in seconds. Making money necessitates quick judgements and a thorough understanding of the strategy being used, but it also necessitates extreme self-control. Without mental discipline, a day trader may make rash decisions, hesitate, or react emotionally, turning prospective profits into losses.

Successful day traders recognize that they compete not just with the market, but also with themselves. Their emotions, biases, and habits heavily influence how they respond to market conditions. It's not enough to simply execute a strategy; they must also manage their own mindset. That is why knowing trading psychology is so important—it allows traders to manage their emotions, decrease stress, and make sensible judgements even when the market is anything but rational.

Important Psychological Challenges in Day Trading

When you first start day trading, you'll rapidly realize that the most difficult challenges are generally internal rather than external. Fear, greed, impatience, and overconfidence are some of the most prevalent psychological obstacles faced by day traders. Each of these emotions, if not managed correctly, can lead to blunders.

Fear: This is one of the strongest emotions in trading. It frequently occurs when a trader feels unsure about their position or suffers a string of losses. This fear can keep individuals from taking action, even when their strategy suggests they should, or it can force them to sell out of a position too soon, foregoing prospective rewards. Learning to recognize and regulate fear is a fundamental aspect of trading psychology.

Greed: Greed can be as harmful as fear. The exhilaration of winning money can lead traders to take undue risks or hold deals for longer than required. This "get-rich-quick" mentality can impair judgement, leading to rash judgements that frequently end in big losses. Greed drives traders to abandon their trading strategies, convincing them that "just one more trade" would result in even greater gains.

Impatience: Patience is essential in day trading, but it is a quality that many people struggle to develop. The market's continuous fluctuation and possibility for profit make it tough to wait for the ideal setup. Impatience causes traders to pursue trades that are not consistent with their strategy, leading to uneven returns.

Success in trading can generate overconfidence,

causing traders to underestimate market risks. Overconfident traders may overlook warning indications, discount the importance of risk management, or aggressively raise their position sizes. This mentality can be perilous, especially in day trading, where one bad choice can wipe out a major portion of one's cash.

Why Psychology Is Important for Consistent Profitability

Every day traders strive for consistency, but it takes more than just a smart strategy to achieve it. Although markets are unpredictable, a trader's mindset can be consistent. A disciplined, patient, and emotionally balanced trader is more likely to make sound decisions, stick to their strategy, and avoid costly errors. Consistency in trading psychology translates into consistent performance.

The secret to good day trading is to stick to a strategy and manage risks properly, rather than being correct all the time. Day trading psychology advises traders to concentrate on long-term benefits rather than quick wins or losses. Traders can avoid having a few bad transactions affect their mindset or future judgements by controlling their emotions and remaining disciplined. This is what distinguishes continuously profitable traders from others who quickly burn out or have major financial failures.

What You Will Learn from This Book

Throughout this book, we will look at the psychological components of day trading that all traders must understand. We'll look at how to develop emotional discipline, handle stress, and remain focused in the face of market turbulence. You'll discover how to spot emotional triggers and cultivate a mindset that supports your trading objectives.

This tour will cover anxiety management measures, how to prevent impulsive trades, and the value of reflection and review. As you continue, you'll learn practical strategies for developing a resilient mindset, overcoming psychological barriers, and improving your ability to maintain control. We'll also talk about intuition and adaptability, which become increasingly vital as you gain trading expertise.

The purpose of this book is to provide you with methods to deal with the ups and downs of trading without allowing emotions to get in the way. Mastering the mental game allows you to lay the groundwork for sustained profitability and long-term progress.

Path to Mental Mastery in Day Trading

In day trading, you will experience both triumph and doubt. It is normal to feel highs when your transactions go well and lows when the market swings against you. The idea is to establish a psychological foundation that will keep you stable, confident, and resilient no matter what happens. By focusing on cultivating the appropriate mindset, you'll be better equipped to face obstacles and seize opportunities with confidence.

Remember that becoming a successful day trader requires ongoing self-improvement. You'll focus on refining your mental approach over time, just as you would with a strategy or a technical indicator. This book will walk you through the process of understanding your thoughts and emotions in the context of day trading. You will not only improve your trading skills, but also grow as a person capable of thriving in a demanding, dynamic atmosphere.

Mastering the mental game of day trading entails gaining self-control, managing emotions, and learning to thrive under pressure. Let us embark on this adventure to lay the psychological basis for consistent earnings and long-term success in the field of day trading.

Chapter One

Developing Emotional Discipline

Mastering the technical aspects of trading is simply one part of the process. The emotional side of trading is a very separate story; most traders overlook it when they start. Many traders find that their biggest challenges aren't recognizing market movements, but rather managing their emotions. Emotional discipline is one of the most important talents a trader can develop; it refers to the capacity to remain cool, focused, and consistent in the face of market volatility.

Recognize Emotional Triggers

Every trader experiences their own set of emotional triggers. Some gamblers are motivated by the fear of losing money, while others are motivated by the pleasure of winning big. The first step in learning emotional discipline is realizing these triggers. A trigger can be any scenario or incident that elicits strong emotions and leads to rash decision-making. For example, some traders become worried and overly cautious following a major loss, forcing them to abandon trades prematurely. Others may get excited when they discover a favorable scenario and rush in without double-checking their plan.

When I started trading, I recall being frustrated and anxious to recoup my losses. I would instinctively initiate a trade when I noticed a slight upward movement, only to discover later that my decision was driven purely by the need to "win back" my losses. Each time I did this, I wound up more in debt. It took some time, but I finally realized that my fear of losing clouded my judgment. Recognizing this pattern allowed me to begin developing a strategy for dealing with it.

Managing Fear and Greed in Trading

Fear and greed are the two primary emotions that influence traders, frequently leading to irrational decisions. Fear can keep you from making trades when you should, and greed can lead you to take needless risks. Understanding these emotions is critical since they are normal reactions that everyone has. The goal is to regulate these feelings so that they do not interfere with your trading strategy.

Fear frequently manifests itself in the form of hesitation. You may analyze a setup, and see a terrific opportunity, but have a nagging uncertainty that prevents you from entering the trade. Perhaps you've lately suffered a loss and are concerned that the following trade will be similarly unsuccessful. The difficulty is that this hesitation can lead to missed opportunities, and missing out on possible advantages can further damage your confidence. Fear can sometimes lead you to exit trades early. When the market goes against you even a little, fear may set in, causing you to cut your losses too soon.

On the other hand, greed often emerges following a string of good trades. You may begin to feel invincible, believing that you cannot lose. This overconfidence may cause you to expand your position or ignore your typical risk management methods. Greed can cause you to cling onto winning trades for too long, expecting even larger returns, only for the market to reverse abruptly, wiping out your winnings. Fear and greed both have the potential to disrupt your strategy, therefore it is critical to be conscious of their impact on your decisions.

Staying Emotionally Neutral

Emotional neutrality entails approaching the market objectively, and treating successes and losses as part of the game. This does not imply that you should not be glad when you win or unhappy when you lose; rather, you should respond in a way that does not influence your next play. Experienced traders realize that each trade is a unique event that should not impact subsequent trades.

Consider placing a trade that first works in your favor but then begins to reverse. A rookie trader may panic and close the trade immediately, fearing a loss. In contrast, a disciplined trader would stick to their plan. They recognize that slight variations are unavoidable and that risk management is more essential than responding emotionally to every small change. By remaining emotionally neutral, you allow your strategy, not your emotions, to direct your decisions.

Practical Techniques for Developing Emotional Discipline

Developing emotional discipline requires practice and self-awareness. One excellent strategy is to create a habit that mentally prepares you before you begin trading. This could be evaluating your trading strategy, making specific goals for the day, or simply practicing a short meditation session to clear your mind. Starting the day with focus and tranquility will allow you to approach trading with a clear mind.

Another effective strategy is journaling. After each trading session, take a few moments to reflect on your trades. Record not only the technical details but also your emotions during each trade. Did you feel nervous? Excited? Anxious? Noticing these feelings can indicate trends that influence your decision-making. By becoming aware of these emotional cues, you can eventually learn to detach from them.

A third strategy is to establish precise guidelines to safeguard oneself from impulsive behavior. For example, if you know you tend to overtrade following a loss, place a limit on the number of trades you can make every day. Once you've reached your limit, exit the market. This rule will help you stick to your strategy and avoid trading out of irritation or desperation.

The Long-Term Advantages of Emotional Discipline

Developing emotional discipline is a slow process, but the long-term advantages are immeasurable. As you gain discipline, your trading decisions will become clearer and less reactive. You will feel more in control, regardless of market conditions. This mental resilience not only improves your trading performance, but it also provides a sense of stability and confidence that may be transferred to other aspects of your life.

When you control your emotions, you are better able to withstand the highs and lows of day trading without letting them distort your judgment. You'll begin to consider each trade as part of a wider journey, knowing that wins and losses do not define you as a trader. Instead, what defines you is your capacity to remain focused, stick to your strategy, and continuously improve.

In the following chapters, we'll go deeper into the mental side of trading, including tactics for stress management, increased focus, and developing the mental resilience required to survive in the fast-paced world of day trading. Each chapter will give you methods to improve your mental game, allowing you to become a more productive and consistent trader over time.

Chapter Two

Developing Confidence and Resilience.

In day trading, confidence and resilience are essential attributes. Confidence in your strategy keeps you grounded during unpredictable market moves, while resilience enables you to recover from setbacks. Without these attributes, even the strongest technical analysis skills will be ineffective in the long run. Developing a mindset that can handle both wins and losses without being overly emotional is what distinguishes successful traders from those who burn out.

The Importance of Confidence in Day Trading

Trading with confidence does not imply that you will win every trade. Instead, it is a consistent trust in your approach, strategy, and ability to make great decisions over time. Many rookie traders gain confidence after a few wins, but this confidence is usually fleeting and can be readily damaged by a loss. True confidence comes from establishing a solid knowledge basis, developing a tried-and-true strategy, and acquiring market experience.

I vividly remember my first trading day, when my confidence fluctuated with my outcomes. If I had a few winning trades, I'd be ecstatic, certain that I'd "figured it out." However, a spate of losses would follow, and that confidence would disintegrate almost instantly. One day, following a particularly difficult losing run, I realized that my confidence was dependent on the success of each trade. I hadn't yet learned to trust my strategy or faith in my ability to remain disciplined even during difficult times.

Building actual confidence took time, and I had to step away from certain trades to focus on the long-term approach. I discovered that confidence isn't something that just "happens" once you make money. It is something you develop through experience and discipline. With time, I began to trust my strategy and realized that each trade was just one step in a much broader journey.

Staying Resilient Following Losses

Losses are an unavoidable aspect of trading. Even the best traders experience losing streaks. The resilience of those who succeed distinguishes them from those who give up. Resilience is the ability to persevere, modify adapt, and learn from each loss, rather than allowing it to shake your confidence or cause self-doubt. It's an important ability because, in trading, emotional recovery from a loss is frequently more difficult than financial recovery.

When I first experienced a severe loss, I felt as though the wind had been knocked out of me. I remember staring at my screen, contemplating every action that had brought me here, and wondering if I was even made out for trading. That day, I was close to giving up. Instead of resigning, I resolved to do an objective analysis of what went wrong. I examined the trade without allowing my fury to take over, asking myself what I might learn from it. This practice of carefully analyzing my losses became a habit over time, and it assisted me in developing resilience. Rather than viewing each loss as a setback to my self-esteem, I began to consider them as learning experiences.

How to Develop Lasting Confidence and Resilience

Building confidence and resilience does not happen overnight. It demands dedication and a willingness to learn, even from trades that are against you. Here are some techniques to help you develop these qualities:

Embrace a Growth Mindset: Traders with a growth mindset think that their skills will improve with time and effort. They see each trade, win or loss as an opportunity to learn. This mindset is essential for developing resilience because it encourages you to view setbacks as a natural part of the learning process rather than signals of failure.

Focus on Process Over Outcome: Learning to detach from individual results and focus on the process is one of the most difficult aspects of trading. Rather than merely celebrating successful trades, begin to value every trade that was done as planned, regardless of the outcome. Over time, focusing on procedure rather than quick rewards will help you gain confidence in your ability to be focused and stick to your strategy.

Create a Reflection Routine: Reflection is an extremely effective technique for personal growth. After each trading day, spend a few minutes reviewing your trades. Have you followed your strategy? Were there any instances when you acted out of fear or greed? Keeping a trading notebook can be extremely useful in spotting patterns in your behavior. This frequent exercise can help you become more aware of your strengths and flaws, which is essential for developing confidence over time.

Importance of Bouncing Back

Recovering from a loss is more than just moving on; it's about actively learning from the experience so you can be better prepared the next time. One of the most common mistakes traders make is allowing a single loss to shake their confidence. For example, following a lost trade, some traders would make hasty trades in an attempt to "win back" their losses. This "revenge trading" rarely ends well because it is motivated by emotions rather than strategy.

Instead, let yourself have time to process each loss. Take a break if necessary, but remember to return to the market with a clear mind. Examine the loss objectively and ask yourself if you could have done anything differently. Perhaps the loss was due to market volatility rather than a mistake on your part, or perhaps you overlooked a point in your research. In any case, instead of allowing the experience to shake your confidence, use it to improve your approach.

Maintaining Balance Throughout Winning Streaks

Losses can test your resilience, but winning streaks test your discipline and humility. It's tempting to become overconfident following a string of winning trades, but this may be just as detrimental as losing confidence. Overconfidence frequently prompts traders to expand their position sizes or enter trades that do not satisfy their customary criteria, resulting in unanticipated losses.

A mentor of mine once told me to approach every trade as if it were my first. He stated that by keeping a "beginner's mindset," I could remain humble and cautious even after winning. This technique has been useful in keeping my confidence stable rather than allowing it to grow with each victory. It reminds me that the market is unpredictable and that discipline and humility are essential.

Building Long-term Confidence and Resilience

Confidence and resilience in day trading do not imply being fearless or expecting to win every trade. They're about trusting your approach, adhering to your strategy, and recovering from setbacks. Developing these traits requires time and effort, but the benefits are great. A confident, resilient trader is better able to cope with market volatility, recover from losses, and maintain long-term profitability.

As you continue on your journey, remember that developing confidence and resilience is an ongoing process. Each trade, win, and loss is an opportunity to strengthen these skills. By focusing on growth, accepting each experience, and remaining committed to improvement, you will develop the mental toughness required to succeed in the difficult world of day trading.

Chapter Three

Mastering Focus and Concentration

Focus and concentration are essential for all traders, but they are more important for day traders. The fast speed and intense pressure of day trading may quickly overwhelm even seasoned traders, so remaining mentally sharp is essential for making accurate, timely decisions. However, staying focused is frequently easier said than done. The temptation of distractions, the stress of continuously changing markets, and the psychological weight of each decision may all derail concentration. In this chapter, we'll look at how to improve your focus and concentration in trading, and why it's one of the most valuable talents a day trader can have.

The Advantages of Mental Clarity in Trading

When you're completely focused on the topic at hand, you can absorb information faster, notice things you'd otherwise overlook, and make better, more sensible decisions. In trading, a lack of concentration can result in missed opportunities or uncalculated risks. This is especially critical for day traders, who frequently work on short timescales and must respond fast to market fluctuations.

I remember a trade early in my career where I lost my focus for a few minutes, but it was enough to transform what could have been a lucrative trade into a little loss. I'd been watching a currency pair as it approached a support level all morning. When it finally reached that level, I became distracted by emails, and by the time I returned to my chart, the pair had already bounced off support and moved in the direction I expected. I missed my perfect entrance, and despite my efforts to catch up with the trade, I ended up entering at a less advantageous position and had to settle for a lower profit. That experience showed me the importance of being totally present and avoiding distractions.

Techniques for Staying Mentally Sharp

Maintaining mental sharpness in trading necessitates a proactive attitude. Here are some useful techniques for keeping your mind focused and awake throughout trading sessions:

Create a Clear Pre-Trading Routine:
Traders can gain from a mental warm-up, just like sportsmen do before a competition. A pre-trading

ritual allows you to get into the appropriate mindset, focus on your goals, and minimize distractions before you start trading. This practice could include evaluating your trading plan, going over your critical levels for the day, or taking a few minutes to meditate to clear your mind. The goal is to create a ritual that prepares you psychologically and physically to fully participate in the market.

Take Regular Breaks: It may seem contradictory, but taking small breaks during your trading session will help you stay focused. Our brains are not built to retain intense concentration for extended periods of time, and weariness can lead to errors. A brief five-minute break every hour to stretch or take a few deep breaths will help you refresh your mind and return to the screen with renewed focus.

Practice mindfulness Techniques: Mindfulness exercises can be quite useful for traders. Being mindful means paying attention to your ideas without passing judgement and remaining in the present. If your mind wanders or you feel yourself becoming stressed, take a moment to concentrate. Try techniques like deep breathing or body scanning, which involve bringing awareness to each region of your body and calming it as you go. These exercises help you focus on the present moment and eliminate mental clutter, helping you to concentrate more on your trades.

Reduce External Distractions: When trading, strive to create a distraction-free atmosphere. This could include shutting your phone, turning off notifications, or even creating a distinct trading area where you will not be distracted. If possible, refrain from checking emails or engaging in other activities during trading hours. Each distraction that takes your focus away from the screen increases the likelihood of missing critical information or making an error.

Avoiding Distractions in a Stressful Environment

Market volatility can create a high-stress environment, making it difficult to stay focused. Distractions can arise from both external and internal sources, such as the phone ringing or an overwhelming desire to check your account balance every few minutes. Both forms of distractions can disrupt your concentration and result in poor decision-making.

I made it a habit to continually review my open positions. Every minor change in profit and loss caught my attention, distracting me from my trading strategy and causing unnecessary stress. I'd open a trade and quickly refresh my computer to check if I was making or losing money. Not only did this habit prevent me from focusing on other chances, but it also contributed to a cycle of anxiety since I was too focused on short-term wins and losses rather than the big picture.

Over time, I learnt not to micromanage my trades. Now, I create alerts for important levels and only revisit my trades at regular intervals, trusting my plan above my emotions. This move has allowed me to avoid distractions and focus on my overall strategy.

Recognize when to hold back.

Learning when to hold back is one of the hardest problems for day traders. The fast-paced environment can create a sense of urgency, leading some traders to enter trades impulsively in order to stay active in the market. This impulse can be hazardous, especially if it leads to overtrading or entering low-probability positions.

Knowing when to hold back needs both self-awareness and discipline. If you find yourself wanting to enter a trade without a clear setup or begin taking trades outside of your strategy, take a step back and ask yourself why. Are you trying to make a profit or are you just bored? Do you feel pressure to "make up" for a recent loss? Recognizing these urges is essential for keeping discipline and concentrating solely on high-quality setups.

Sticking to a well-thought-out plan

A solid trading plan is one of the most effective instruments for maintaining focus and self-control. Your strategy serves as a road map, guiding you through various market conditions and helping you avoid making rash decisions. When you have a well-thought-out strategy in place, you are less likely to be influenced by emotions or distracted by market noise.

Think of your trading strategy as a checklist. Before each trade, ask yourself if it satisfies the requirements in your plan. If it doesn't, it's a good sign that the trade is motivated by emotions rather than analysis. This method has greatly aided me over the years. Having a plan allows me to trade with confidence, knowing that each decision is based on careful consideration and study.

Developing a Long-Term Focus for Consistent Results.

Developing focus and concentration does not happen overnight. It's a skill that takes consistent practice and a desire to grow. Just like athletes practice every day to improve their performance, traders must actively focus on staying mentally sharp and eliminating distractions. Over time, your efforts will pay off as you find yourself making more sensible, consistent decisions, resulting in more steady trading results.

Remember that keeping focused in trading is more than just avoiding distractions; it is also about developing the ability to stay present, manage impulses, and make decisions that are consistent with your strategy. By investing in these abilities, you will create a more disciplined trading style that will support your long-term success.

Chapter Four

Impulse Control and Overtrading.

Impulse control is one of the most important talents in day trading. In a field where decisions must frequently be made rapidly, the ability to distinguish between impulsive drives and sensible choices might mean the difference between constant earnings and increasing losses. Overtrading, a widespread problem among both new and seasoned traders, is generally caused by a lack of impulse control. In this chapter, we will look at tactics for recognizing impulsive behavior, learning to hold back when appropriate, and developing the discipline to keep to a well-thought-out plan.

Understanding the Urge to Act on Impulse.

Day trading may be exciting. The market's pace, profit potential, and rapid influx of fresh information all contribute to an environment that can elicit powerful emotional responses. For many traders, this excitement can lead to impulsive decisions, such as entering trades without a clear justification, raising position sizes in order to "make up" for a past loss, or acting on a whim because they don't want to miss out.

I recall a period early in my trading career when I became stuck in this pattern. After a particularly good day, I was on a high, feeling invincible. I assumed I had a flawless understanding of the market and kept entering trades that didn't fit my regular criteria, believing I'd keep winning. My spate of impulsive trades quickly turned into losses, wiping out the entire day's winnings and then some. I let my emotions to take precedence over my strategy, and it cost me dearly. This event showed me the value of sticking to my trading plan and recognizing minor signals that my decisions were influenced by impulse rather than strategy.

Dangers of Overtrading

Over-trading is one of the most typical mistakes in day trading. It occurs when traders place too many trades in a short period of time, frequently under pressure to remain active or make up for recent losses. This behavior can lead to decreased focus, high transaction costs, and poor decision-making. Overtrading can transform a perfectly planned strategy into a chaotic succession of hurried moves, resulting in rapid losses.

Overtrading has a variety of causes. Some traders are compelled to always "do something" in the market, believing that the more they trade, the more money they will make. Others may overtrade in response to a loss, trying to recover fast by entering fresh positions. However, rather than being a reaction to emotions or external forces, each trade should serve a definite objective and be aligned with a clear setup. The truth is that trading more does not imply trading better.

Developing Patience and Knowing When to Hold Back

One of the most difficult things in trading is learning to wait. Knowing when not to trade is equally crucial as knowing when to trade. Successful traders learn patience and recognize that waiting on the sidelines is frequently the best option. There will be days when market conditions are not favorable to your strategy, and forcing trades at these periods can lead to unneeded losses.

Patience may be extremely difficult, particularly in the fast-paced world of day trading. There's a natural yearning to participate, to be "doing something." However, trading is as much about waiting for the proper conditions as it is about taking action. If you feel compelled to enter a trade without a clear rationale, take a step back. Consider whether this decision is motivated by impatience or whether it corresponds with your trading strategy. Stepping away from the screen or taking a little break can help you reset and refocus.

I learnt this lesson the hard way. During a particularly tumultuous trading session, I noticed possibilities everywhere. I continued jumping in, convinced that if I wasn't trading, I was missing out. In actuality, my hasty decisions were causing me to lose control of my strategy. After that day, I realized that more trades didn't always equal more success. Actually, the reverse was true. From that point on, I began establishing explicit criteria for each trade and forcing myself to wait until those criteria were met, regardless of what the market was doing.

Sticking to a well-thought-out plan

Your trading strategy is your most powerful weapon against impulsive decisions and overtrading. A solid plan outlines your strategy, entry and exit points, risk management criteria, and trade conditions for each transaction. By using a planned approach, you are less likely to act on impulse and more likely to make decisions that align with your objectives.

A well-designed trading plan provides clarity and discipline, but it only works if you stick to it. This necessitates fighting the temptation to make decisions on a whim, no matter how strong the desire. When you have a trading strategy, you can approach each trade with purpose and confidence, rather than allowing emotions to guide your decisions.

A mentor recently told me that a trading plan is like a compass, keeping you on track even when the market turns unexpected. Since that day, I've treated my plan with the same regard that I would give a map on an unfamiliar trail. If I find myself drifting off course, I refer back to my strategy to figure out where I went wrong. This habit has saved me countless times from chasing trades that did not satisfy my criteria, so avoiding excessive losses.

Practical Strategies for Impulse Control.

Impulse control in trading is a skill that may be improved with practice and awareness. Here are some practical ways to help you control your impulses and avoid overtrading:

Set Daily Trade Limits: Before you begin trading, determine the maximum amount of trades you will make per day. This limit drives you to be more discerning about the trades you make, which helps you avoid impulsive decisions and overtrading. For example, you may opt to only make three trades every day. When you've reached this limit, take a break and analyze your trades rather than chasing new opportunities.

Use a Trading Journal: Keeping a trading journal can be an effective tool for controlling impulses. After each trading day, keep track of your trades, thoughts, and emotions. Patterns will form over time that will show your triggers for impulsive decisions. By being aware of these patterns, you will be better able to control your reactions and make deliberate, controlled decisions.

Implement the "Pause" Rule: If you feel compelled to enter a trade that is not part of your strategy, pause for a few moments and take a deep breath. Allow yourself time to analyze the situation objectively. If the trade corresponds with your strategy or if you are reacting emotionally, ask yourself. Often, a quick pause is enough to help you recognize and resist impulsive feelings.

Practice Visualization: Before you begin

trading each day, envision yourself following your plan with discipline, making calculated decisions, and avoiding impulsive behavior. Visualization might help you mentally prepare to behave with control and patience. You can reinforce your resolve to avoiding impulse-driven decisions by mentally practicing excellent trading habits.

Maintaining Long-term Discipline for Consistent Profits

In the long run, maintaining impulse control and avoiding overtrading are critical to sustainable profitability. Trading is not about taking constant action; it is about taking measured risks and waiting for high-quality opportunities. Traders who approach the market with discipline and resist the impulse to respond on passing emotions are more likely to succeed in the long run.

Remember that every decision you make affects your long-term progress. You'll develop a more solid, reliable approach to day trading by learning to control your impulses, sticking to a trade plan, and resisting the need to overtrade. These behaviors will eventually become second nature, allowing you to trade with clarity, confidence, and consistency.

Chapter Five

Managing Anxiety and Trading Pressure

Anxiety is a normal component of trading. With every decision having the potential for profit or loss, the pressure to perform is intense, and even the most experienced traders are not immune to emotional stress. The market's continual ups and downs can cause concern, particularly when trades do not go as anticipated, and the necessity to make quick decisions can exacerbate stress. However, managing anxiety efficiently is critical for day traders. Those who can remain calm under pressure make better decisions, handle risk more efficiently, and achieve more consistent outcomes.

In this chapter, we'll look at the causes of trading

anxiety, how it affects performance, and how to keep calm and collected even when the market seems to be testing every nerve.

Understanding the Causes of Trading Anxiety

Trading anxiety is often caused by the large risks involved in each decision. When investing money, the potential for loss lurks over every decision, which can lead to emotions based on fear. Traders often confront time constraints, knowing that a missed chance could result in a lost reward. Even successful traders might have performance anxiety, which is caused by a fear of failing to live up to previous triumphs or losing a winning run. During one of my first large trading weeks, I can still clearly recall my anxiety. I had a run of wins that left me feeling both excited and terrified—I didn't want to lose the progress I'd made. But that fear gradually turned into pressure, and I began second-guessing my decisions, hesitating on trades that I would have made confidently otherwise. The anxiety took control, and I ended up quitting positions prematurely and bypassing certain high-probability setups because I was afraid of interrupting my winning streak. That experience taught me that anxiety might impair my judgement just as much as market noise.

The Effects of Anxiety on Decision Making

Anxiety, if unmanaged, can lead to rash decisions, reluctance, or avoidance, all of which can be detrimental to trading performance. When you're anxious, your brain switches into "fight or flight" mode, and rational decision-making takes a second seat to instinctive impulses. For traders, this frequently results in either leaping into trades out of fear of missing out or freezing up and missing out entirely.

The difficulty with anxiety-driven decisions is that they are rarely founded on solid reasoning. Instead, they are responses to perceived anxieties, such as loss, failure, or regret. These emotions may be valid, but they are not reliable trading indicators. Learning to handle anxiety allows you to think more clearly and make decisions based on your strategy rather than the fleeting emotions that anxiety causes.

Techniques to Stay Calm and Collected

Fortunately, there are techniques that might help you reduce anxiety and stay focused during trading sessions. *Here are a few that I've found to be especially useful:*

Practice Deep Breathing: Deep breathing is one of the most basic and efficient strategies to calm your anxiety. When you're anxious, your body generally responds with short, fast breaths, which further worsens the panic feeling. Slow, deep breathing helps stimulate your body's relaxation response, allowing you to feel more calm and centered. Before each trading session, I close my eyes and take deep, purposeful breaths for a few minutes. It's a little practice, but it establishes a sense of calm that I can return to whenever I feel anxiety coming in.

Set Clear Risk Limits: One common source of anxiety in trading is the fear of losing too much money on a single trade. You can reduce this fear by setting and adhering to defined risk limits. Knowing how much you're willing to lose in a trade provides you control and lowers uncertainty. It also emphasizes that, while losses are conceivable, they are within controllable boundaries. When I began setting rigorous risk limitations, I noticed that my anxiety decreased significantly because I no longer thought I was "gambling" with my money.

Create a Routine to Ground Yourself:

Routines are effective aids for staying focused and minimizing stress. When you stick to a consistent pre-trading routine, like as reviewing your strategy, reading the news, or setting up your charts, your brain knows you're prepared. This practice boosts confidence while eliminating the sense of unpredictability that frequently causes anxiety. A routine provides structure in a constantly changing environment, which can be comforting.

Focus on Process, Not Outcome: Many traders feel worried because they are excessively focused on the consequences of specific trades. They think in terms of wins and losses, with each trade representing their ability. Instead of focusing on the outcome, it is better to focus on the process. Each trade should be viewed as a single step in a wider strategy. By understanding trading as a process, you may shift the focus away from individual results and reduce the pressure on each trade to succeed. This mental shift can help you remain calm even during stressful sessions.

Recognizing and Reducing Stress

Stress is unavoidable in trading, but it does not need to be overpowering. Recognizing the indications of stress—racing thoughts, muscle tension, and irritability—can help you detect it early and take actions to control it before it affects your trading decisions.

I've discovered that taking a little break during the day can be really beneficial. When I feel nervous or my mind is racing, I step away from my desk for a few minutes. Whether it's a quick stroll or just stretching, this break allows me to refocus. I return to my screen with a clearer mind, prepared to approach the market more rationally.

Managing Emotions During Winning and Losing Streaks

Winning and losing streaks can cause emotional ups and downs. It's easy to become overconfident after a string of wins, but this exhilaration can lead to riskier behavior and impulsive trades. A streak of losses, on the other hand, can produce dissatisfaction and self-doubt, leading you to forsake your strategy or engage in trades that are not in line with your plan.

The key to dealing with these emotional swings is to remain grounded. One approach to accomplish this is to keep a trading notebook in which you record not just your trades but also your thoughts and feelings. Over time, you'll notice patterns in your emotions and how they link to your trading performance. This self-awareness can help you stay balanced, whether you're winning or losing.

For example, after a particularly lucrative week, I may be tempted to increase my position size or enter trades that do not meet my regular criteria. However, reviewing my notebook reminds me that these emotions are part of a regular cycle, and I can choose to remain disciplined rather than becoming swept away by a fleeting high.

Managing Confidence and Staying Grounded

Confidence is crucial in trading, but it must be anchored on fact. Too little confidence, and you may hesitate, second-guessing every decision; too much, and you may ignore risk. To effectively handle anxiety, maintain a reasonable and consistent degree of confidence.

One way that has helped me is to remind myself that each trade is a separate event. Just because I've lost doesn't indicate the next trade will be a loss, and just because I've won doesn't mean I'll win again. Viewing trades as independent, individual events helps me maintain my confidence, avoid overreactions, and reduce anxiety.

Developing Long-Term Resilience to Anxiety

Managing anxiety and trading pressure is a continuing process that involves constant self-awareness and care. The capacity to handle stress without letting it to influence your trading decisions takes time to master, but the benefits are well worth the effort. Building resilience, creating boundaries, and focusing on process over outcomes will help you develop a trading mindset that can withstand the market's inevitable ups and downs.

Trading is a journey, and anxiety is a normal part of it. Learning to control anxiety not only makes you a better trader, but it also prepares you to face problems in all aspects of your life. Remember that mastering the mental game is what distinguishes consistent traders, and managing anxiety is an important element of that skill. Each session, challenge, and experience will help you become a more calm, focused, and resilient trader.

Chapter Six

Managing Emotions During Winning and Losing Streaks

As day traders, we've experienced both the highs of good trades and the lows of unexpected losses. Winning and losing streaks are unavoidable in trading, but they provide emotional hurdles that can impair judgement and lead to rash decisions. Learning how to regulate emotions during both sorts of streaks is essential for long-term stability. In this chapter, we'll look at strategies for staying balanced, grounded, and objective, no matter what streak we're on.

Emotional Impact of Winning

Streaks

A winning streak is exciting, but it may also be deceiving. A string of wins can build confidence to the point of overconfidence, making traders feel nearly invincible. It is easy to forget that the market is unpredictable, and that each trade is a separate event with its own set of dangers. This inflated confidence can lead to greater positions, more aggressive strategies, and, in many cases, a departure from one's typical trading plan.

I remember a time in my trading career when I had a streak of profitable trades. I was on a roll, and with each good trade, I gained confidence. I quickly increased my trade sizes, confident that I had "cracked the code." However, I was unintentionally departing from my typical risk-management techniques. Eventually, the market turned, and I suffered a substantial loss. That single loss wiped out a significant amount of my profits from the preceding streak. This incident taught me that overconfidence may lead to overextension, and that maintaining grounded is essential—even while on a winning streak.

Avoiding the Trap of Overconfidence

To prevent a winning streak from turning into reckless trading, keep the following strategies in mind:

Stick to Your Risk Parameters: No matter how well you're performing, it's critical to stay inside your initial risk parameters. Winning does not alter the underlying laws of the market, and an unanticipated rise in position size can soon work against you. Maintaining regular risk limits keeps you grounded and avoids the "one big loss" that can undo weeks of hard effort.

Take Time to Reflect: A winning streak provides an excellent time to reflect on what is going well in your trading strategy. Instead of merely celebrating profits, conduct an objective analysis of each trade. Were they all planned out, or did there appear to be impetuous or hazardous decisions? This type of contemplation keeps you in a growing mindset rather than a complacent one, which makes it simpler to maintain balance.

Separate Emotions from Logic: Remind yourself that each trade is a distinct event with its own odds. Even if you've won ten trades in a row, that doesn't mean the following one will be a winner. Approach each trade as a unique opportunity, and don't get caught up in the momentum of previous triumphs. This impartiality will keep your thoughts clear, allowing you to approach each trade with reasonable thought rather than emotional exhilaration.

Managing Emotions during Losing Streaks

In contrast, losing streaks can cause frustration and self-doubt. Losses frequently cause emotions of insecurity, forcing traders to doubt their ability or strategies. When a trader suffers a series of losses, it's normal to desire to "make amends" by engaging in larger, riskier trades to regain lost ground. However, this technique frequently leads to more losses and a downward emotional spiral.

One of the most difficult occasions in my trading career occurred when the market was extremely turbulent. I had a string of losing trades, and with each loss, my confidence eroded. Frustrated, I began to question my method, altering my strategy without clear justification, and engaging in trades that did not fit with my regular plan. I wanted to recoup my losses immediately, but my judgement was distorted by emotion. I eventually saw that I needed to take a step back, regain my composure, and return to the fundamentals of my trading strategy. This experience taught me that sometimes the best course of action after a losing streak is to take a break, reflect, and return to the market with a new perspective.

How to Be Resilient During Losing Streaks

Here are a few ways to efficiently manage your emotions amid a losing streak:

Accept Losses as Part of the Process: Trading involves losses, which cannot be avoided. Accepting this reality can help you approach issues from a more balanced standpoint. Losses should be viewed as market feedback rather than failures. Analyzing these trades allows you to detect any patterns or faults and adapt your strategy accordingly.

Take a Break If Necessary: If you're feeling especially frustrated or emotionally exhausted, it may be time to take a break. Stepping away from the computer for a day or two allows you to process your emotions, clear your mind, and return with renewed focus. Even a short pause has helped me gather perspective and avoid making rash decisions when I've faced challenging losing streaks.

Concentrate on Your Long-Term Strategy: A series of losses does not define your trading career. Remind yourself of your long-term goals and your progress to date. This perspective might help you avoid overreacting to short-term losses and emphasize the significance of maintaining discipline. Successful trading is a marathon, not a sprint, and every trader will experience losses along the road.

Re-evaluate Your Strategy: Following a losing streak, it is a good idea to review your strategy objectively. Were the losses due to weak market conditions, or did you divert from your strategy? Understanding the cause of the losses can provide useful information for future trades. If your strategy is sound, trust it and move forward.

If changes are required, make them carefully and thoughtfully.

Techniques to Stay Grounded

Maintaining an even keel is essential for making effective trading decisions, whether you're on a winning or losing streak. Here are some strategies to help you keep balanced:

Keep a Trading Journal: Recording your trades, emotions, and ideas in a journal can be extremely valuable. You can uncover emotional trends and recognize when you're deviating from a disciplined approach by reviewing your journal. It's also an effective tool for identifying areas for improvement and being self-aware.

Use Visualization Techniques: Visualization is an effective mental tool for preparing for various trading scenarios. Consider how you would react to both a series of wins and a series of losses. Visualizing your reactions might help you deal with certain situations more efficiently when they arise, lowering emotional intensity and keeping you in control.

Mindfulness can help you be present and focused on the here and now, rather than getting caught up in the exhilaration of a winning streak or the frustration of a losing streak. Practicing mindfulness for a few minutes every day can boost your emotional resilience, allowing you to approach each trading session with a clear, focused mind.

Managing Confidence and remaining humble.

Confidence is essential in trading, but it must be balanced with humility. Overconfidence can lead to risky trading, whereas a lack of confidence can result in reluctance and missed opportunities. A proper balance is trusting your abilities and strategy while acknowledging the market's unpredictability.

One of the most important lessons I've learnt is to be humble. The market is a great teacher, and every trader, regardless of expertise, is constantly learning. By respecting the market and remaining open to growth, I've discovered that I can maintain a consistent level of confidence based on reality rather than emotion.

Maintaining Emotional Balance for Long-term Success

Emotional balance is an important aspect of long-term trading success. Winning and losing streaks will come and go, but how you handle these emotional swings will influence your overall performance. By developing emotional awareness, staying grounded, and focusing on consistency over time, you'll be better prepared to deal with the market's inevitable ups and downs.

Remember that trading is much more than just strategies and technical skills; it is also about mastering your mentality. Whether you're on a winning streak or going through a bad patch, keeping a balanced viewpoint will allow you to overcome the hurdles with perseverance, setting the road for consistent, long-term success.

Chapter Seven

Establishing A Growth-Oriented Routine

Success in day trading is about creating and maintaining routines that support continual progress and personal growth, not just about strategies, technical analysis, or market knowledge. Establishing a consistent, growth-oriented routine allows you to approach each trading day with a clear mindset, polished skills, and an objective outlook, making you more prepared to deal with the highs and lows of the trading market.

Importance of Routine in Day Trading

In a volatile environment like the trading market, a systematic routine serves as the foundation for stability. Without a routine, it is easy to slide into reactive trading, which involves making decisions based on emotions or spontaneous impulses rather than clear analysis and strategy. A lack of routine can lead to exhaustion, hasty trades, and variable performance over time.

From personal experience, I've discovered that establishing a daily routine allows me to approach each trading day calmly and prepared. I know exactly how I'll begin the day, what I'll focus on, and how I'll evaluate my success. This structure has allowed me to improve gradually, keep my emotions under control, and maintain consistent progress. A well-defined routine serves as the foundation on which traders can build and perfect their skills, improving both resilience and performance.

Pre-trading preparation

The first step in a growth-oriented routine is to prepare for the market's opening. Taking the time before trading hours to study market circumstances, assess potential opportunities, and psychologically prepare yourself will help you begin the day with clarity.

Review Market News and Trends: Each morning, spend some time reviewing major economic news, worldwide events, and market trends that may affect the day's trading. Checking news sources or economic calendars allows you to predict potential volatility or price swings that may impact your positions.

Set a Clear Intention for the Day: Before getting into trades, I find it helpful to have a precise intention or goal for the day. This could include focusing on risk management, developing patience, or even learning from any mistakes that occur. Setting an intention allows me to approach the market with a sense of purpose, keeping me focused.

Visualize Your Ideal Trading Day:
Visualization is an effective strategy employed by athletes, business leaders, and, yes, successful traders. Take a few minutes to imagine your dream trading day. Consider making calm, informed decisions, sticking to your strategy, and facing any setbacks with resilience. Visualization can help set the tone for the day by reinforcing a focused and collected mindset.

Developing a Midday Check-In

A mid-day check-in is an essential element of a trader's routine, allowing them to reassess the market, examine previous trades, and assess any emotional or mental adjustments. Without this pause, it's easy to keep trading on autopilot or lose track of tiny emotional fluctuations that may be influencing decision making.

Evaluate Morning Trades: Reviewing your

morning trades allows you to reflect on what worked and what didn't. Did you keep to your plans? Did you handle risk successfully? Taking notice of these factors in the middle of the day allows you to make modifications before going forward.

Reset psychologically: Trading is psychologically exhausting, and a mid-day reset might help you stay focused and calm for the rest of the day. Take a little break to step away from the screen, practice deep breathing, or perform a brief mindfulness activity. This moment of pause has been really beneficial to me personally because it prevents mental tiredness and clears my thoughts for the second half of the day.

Reassess the Market: Because markets can shift during the day, it is critical to reassess the environment. Are trends emerging? Is the volatility increasing? Are there any new developments affecting your positions? By monitoring market conditions, you may determine whether to make changes to your strategy or to stick with it.

Post-Trading Reflections

How you conclude your trading day is equally crucial as how you begin it. Post-trading reflections allow you to assess the day's performance, learn from your mistakes, and psychologically prepare for future trades. This reflection process helps me modify my approach and build a growth-oriented mindset, which keeps me interested in continual learning.

Analyze today's trades: Examine each trade you made, whether it was a win or a loss. Determine what went well and where mistakes were made in each step. Was the trade in accordance with your plans? Did you enter or exit due to emotion or analysis? Answering these questions reveals insights that can help you make better decisions in the future.

Document key takeaways: Writing down your thoughts and observations every day is quite beneficial. In my experience, keeping a journal in which I scribble down lessons, emotional responses, and insights has been one of the most beneficial aspects of my routine. Reviewing previous entries reveals patterns and opportunities for growth, serving as a personal guide to continued improvement.

Focus on the Process, Not the Results: Trading success isn't determined by a single day's profits or losses. A growth-oriented routine prioritizes the process—sticking to your plan, staying disciplined, and making wise decisions—over short-term results. Reflecting on whether you followed your process is more beneficial than focusing on the profit or loss of a particular day.

Creating a Routine of Consistency

To build consistency in both performance and mindset, a growth-oriented routine is necessary.

Establishing regular habits that promote learning and growth reduces the impact of emotional highs and lows, allowing you to make more unbiased trading decisions.

Make small improvements every day:
Growth is defined as making modest, incremental improvements every day, rather than making enormous changes. Each morning, I ask myself what one thing I can work on today, whether it's patience, focus, or risk management. Over time, these minor changes add up to tremendous development.

Set Realistic Goals: Having realistic, attainable goals is essential for staying motivated and moving forward. Goals do not have to be profit-oriented; they might be about personal growth, skill advancement, or emotional resilience. You can stay engaged in the learning process without becoming overly focused on outcomes by focusing on growth-oriented goals.

Hold Yourself Accountable: Accountability is an essential component of any routine. In my experience, creating clear goals for myself and sticking to them has helped me become a more disciplined trader. Whether you have a mentor, a trading partner, or simply keep a journal, being able to track your adherence to your routine helps promote beneficial behaviors.

Long-Term Advantages of a Growth-Oriented Routine

A growth-oriented routine focusses on creating a foundation for long-term success as well as enhancing your trades in the short term. By focusing on continual learning and self-improvement, you develop resilience, patience, and adaptability, which will help you navigate the inevitable ups and downs of day trading.

My routine has helped me stay devoted to my trader development over the years. It has provided me with a structure to rely on during difficult times, as well as inspiration when the market tries my commitment. This approach has improved not only my trading performance, but also my mindset, allowing me to see each day as an opportunity for progress.

Embracing growth as a trader

The path to becoming a great day trader has no end point. Adopting a growth-oriented routine keeps you motivated, curious, and resilient. By committing to regular habits of reflection, learning, and progress, you may establish a consistent route to mastery. The process may not always be simple, but it will eventually pay off in terms of trading performance and personal development.

Trading is more than just a series of transactions; it is a discipline, a practice, and an ongoing voyage of self-discovery. A growth-oriented routine ensures that you are building a foundation for long-term trading success rather than just chasing profits.

Chapter Eight

Journaling for Improvement.

One of the most effective skills a trader can develop is the practice of keeping a detailed journal. A trading journal is more than just a record of trades; it's a travel map that includes both wins and losses. By documenting each trading day, a trader can gain insights, detect patterns, and handle the psychological issues that arise during market volatility. A journal can be thought of as your personal coach, encouraging you to self-awareness and progress.

Why Journaling Matters in Day

Trading

Day trading involves fast decisions, shifting emotions, and abrupt market movements. If these experiences are not recorded, they are frequently forgotten, leading you to make the same mistakes. Journaling serves as a link between experience and growth, allowing you to turn day-to-day trades into valuable lessons.

When I first started day trading, I didn't grasp the importance of journaling. I was entirely focused on numbers: profits, losses, and account balance. However, I rapidly saw that without the ability to reflect on and learn from my trades, I was making the same mistakes and missing out on potential for growth. When I committed to keeping a journal, I noticed how much it enhanced my focus and helped me approach each trading day with a mindset based on growth rather than profit.

What to Include in a Trading

Journal?

The success of a trading journal is determined by what you record and how candidly you reflect. A solid journal goes beyond the fundamentals of each trade, delving into the thoughts, feelings, and events that surround them. Here are some important components to include.

Trade Details: Begin with the fundamentals, such as the date, time, asset, entry price, exit price, and trade volume. This information records each trade and helps you to track your success over time.

Market Conditions: Take note of any noteworthy elements that may have influenced your trades, such as market trends, economic news, or levels of volatility. Tracking these factors allows you to see how external events influence your decisions and which contexts you perform best in.

Pre-Trade Emotions and Thoughts: Record how you're feeling before you enter a trade. Are you anxious, excited, or overconfident? Pre-trade emotions frequently affect decisions, and recognizing these patterns allows you to adjust your approach to trading psychology.

Rationale for Entry and Exit: Explain why you joined the trade and why you chose the exit point. This section is crucial for determining whether you adhered to your strategy or acted on impulse. For example, I discovered in my own notebooks that I was abandoning trades prematurely due to fear of loss, indicating a personal tendency of fear-based decision-making.

Post-Trade Reflection: After the trade, consider what went correctly and poorly. Have you followed your strategy? Were there any unexpected factors? How did you feel following the trade: relieved, regretful, or indifferent? Over time, these reflections demonstrate how emotions such as fear and greed influence your outcomes.

Lessons learnt: Finally, consider the essential takeaway from each trade. This could be a reminder to follow a rule you ignored, an understanding of your emotional triggers, or a realization about the efficacy of a particular strategy. Reviewing these lessons helps you develop as a trader and build a mindset that is focused on progress.

The Effects of Journaling on Emotional Awareness

Journaling gives traders a unique opportunity to examine their emotions. Because they are viewed as flaws, traders are often hesitant to express feelings of fear, greed, or frustration. However, knowing and accepting these emotions is essential to become a disciplined trader.

For example, I remember a series of trades in

which I impulsively entered the market after watching a few winning trades. I'd have overconfidence, leading me to take larger risks without a strong rationale, only to suffer major losses shortly thereafter. Writing about these instances encouraged me to address my impulsive behavior, particularly after a winning streak. It also offered me the opportunity to practice strategies to combat this behavior, such as taking a five-minute break after each trade to reset emotionally.

Using Journaling to Find Patterns and Improve Strategies

Another significant advantage of journaling is that it allows traders to see patterns in their trading behavior and strategy performance. Reviewing journal entries over time reveals insights that are difficult to detect otherwise, helping you refine your trading approach and tackle reoccurring issues.

Pattern Recognition: When reviewing journal entries, seek for common themes in your trades. Are there any special circumstances under which you tend to excel or struggle? Are specific times of day more suited to your trading style? Identifying patterns allows you to adjust your strategies to better fit with your strengths.

Refining Strategies: Journaling enables you to test and refine strategies using a data-driven approach. For example, if a specific strategy frequently results in losses, a review of your journal can tell whether the problem is with the strategy or its implementation. I've personally rejected strategies that routinely produced bad results and tweaked others to better suit my approach, all owing to feedback from my journal.

Evaluating Emotional Triggers: If you notice patterns in your emotional responses, such as feeling apprehensive before entering specific trades, you can address them proactively. My journal helped me recognize which volatile market settings were more likely to induce emotional stress, which led me to avoid certain setups when I wasn't in the appropriate mindset.

Long-term Benefits of Journaling

Journaling is an investment in yourself and your trader growth. It is not a quick fix, but it can be used over time to promote growth and ongoing improvement. By keeping a daily journal, you give yourself the opportunity to learn, adapt, and grow with each trade.

Increasing Self-Awareness: The more you journal, the more you'll understand your inclinations, strengths, and flaws. This self-awareness is extremely valuable in day trading, where personal discipline can make the difference between success and failure.

Tracking Progress Over Time: One of the most satisfying features of journaling is being able to reflect on how far you've come. In moments of doubt or frustration, reviewing previous entries reveals progress made and lessons learnt, providing motivation and perspective.

Creating Accountability: Journaling holds you accountable to your goals and routines. It's easy to deviate from a trading strategy or disregard mistakes when there's no record of them, but a journal holds you accountable by documenting each decision and the consequence.

Developing Your Own Journaling Routine

Starting a journal can seem intimidating, but it doesn't have to be. The idea is to develop a method that works for you and make a commitment to utilizing it regularly. Whether you prefer a digital platform or a physical notebook, select a format that is suitable for you. Set aside time at the conclusion of each trading day for evaluation, and remember that the goal is not perfection, but growth.

When I first started journaling, I kept it simple, recording only the essential data and a few observations. As I became more comfortable, I included areas for emotional analysis and strategy appraisal. Today, my journal has become an essential part of my trading routine, and the insights it gives are critical to my continued progress.

Accepting Journaling as a Path to Growth

Journaling isn't about repeating mistakes or focusing on losses; it's about adopting a growth mindset. By documenting each trade with honesty and transparency, you develop a road map for continual progress. You gain knowledge, refine your strategies, and build a mental toolset for long-term success with each entry.

Through journaling, you may turn each trading day into an opportunity for learning and growth. It becomes more than just a record of previous trades; it's a diary of your trip, development, and evolution as a trader. Your journal is there to assist you, helping you learn from the past and build a brighter future in the world of day trading, whether you're riding a high or navigating a difficult market.

Chapter Nine

Setting Realistic Profit Goals.

Setting reasonable profit targets is critical in day trading, because the rush of quick gains can lead traders to have unrealistic expectations. Creating attainable, progressive goals acts as both a guide and a safeguard, helping traders remain grounded and avoid the emotional traps that might develop when pursuing unattainable profits. Goals should focus not just on profit, but also on consistency and personal growth, as these are the foundation for long-term success.

Why Do Realistic Goals Matter?

In the fast-paced world of day trading, it's easy to get caught up in the prospect of large, quick profits. Many traders enter the market with the hope of doubling or even tripling their account within months, only to experience disappointment and frustration when reality does not live up to their expectations. This is when realistic goal setting comes into play. Setting attainable goals helps traders construct a manageable route to success and reduces the likelihood of making impulsive decisions.

When I first started day trading, I had huge expectations and set lofty profit targets that were unreasonable given my level of knowledge. Inevitably, I found myself taking more risks to accomplish those ambitions, which resulted in a string of losses. Frustration grew, and I realized my approach was untenable. My trading only stabilized and I started to see actual success when I made the shift to setting smaller, incremental goals. This experience showed me that consistent growth was more valuable—and more attainable—than aiming for massive profits.

Breaking Down Profit Goals.

The first step in defining realistic profit targets is to divide them down into smaller, more manageable chunks. Instead of creating an annual objective, consider starting with weekly or monthly targets that are consistent with your strategy and account size. This approach makes goals less intimidating and allows for frequent reflection and change.

Weekly Goals: Setting weekly goals allows you to keep focused on short-term performance while avoiding overwhelm. For example, if you aim for a small 1-2% weekly gain, this might mount up over time while keeping risks under control. Weekly goals offer for faster feedback, allowing you to evaluate what's working and what needs to be altered right away.

Monthly Goals: After you've established a

weekly rhythm, consider setting monthly aims that reflect bigger patterns and modifications. Monthly goals allow you to evaluate performance and make larger modifications to your strategy as necessary. A monthly goal should include both winning and losing weeks in order to ensure steady improvement.

Long-Term Goals: While short-term goals are essential, setting a long-term vision is also beneficial. This could be a six-month or year goal based on conservative forecasts. Long-term objectives should prioritize stability and skill development, with the goal of making steady progress rather than immediate wins.

Focusing on Incremental Growth

Consistent, incremental growth is essential in day trading for building confidence and capital. Focus on little, consistent wins that add up over time rather than striving for a home run with each trade. This approach decreases the psychological pressure to perform, allowing you to make more reasoned, disciplined decisions.

My mindset transformed substantially when I began to focus on incremental growth. Instead of feeling pressured to earn a high profit every day, I focused on making sound trades that were consistent with my strategy. This shift lessened the emotional highs and lows associated with overreaching. Setting realistic targets made it easier for me to stick to my plan and improve my trading consistency.

Balancing Profit Goals and Skill Development

Setting profit targets is crucial, but they should not be the primary focus. Develop your trade skills. Risk management, strategy refinement, and emotional control are the building blocks of success, and focusing on them will help you achieve your profit targets.

Risk management: This is an important ability to develop. Understanding and establishing appropriate risk limits per trade is essential since it protects your capital and lessens the impact of losses. For example, if you want to make a 1% profit every week, limit each trade to a maximum loss of 0.5% of your account. This discipline maintains your trades within a realistic risk level, allowing you to avoid significant drawdowns.

Strategy Refinement: As you move towards your profit objectives, take the time to refine your strategy using journaled notes and trade comments. Pay attention to which settings are most effective, and adjust your strategy accordingly. This continuous improvement process supports the goal of incremental growth and guarantees that your approach remains effective over time.

Emotional Control: Managing emotions is possibly the most difficult skill to acquire, but it is also one of the most rewarding. Maintaining discipline in the face of losses—or wins—may be difficult, but setting realistic goals can help to balance emotional swings. When you know your goal is attainable, you're less likely to act out of fear or greed, which are frequently the most significant barriers to achievement.

Recognizing and adjusting unrealistic expectations.

Setting realistic goals entails being willing to adjust as market conditions or personal circumstances change. Markets are unpredictable, and adhering to goals that no longer represent reality can lead to bad decision-making.

I set profit targets that were unrealistic given the market conditions at the time. When the market became erratic, I attempted to force my trades to achieve targets, which simply increased my losses. It took me a long to realize that being adaptable to my goals was a sign of strength, not weakness. Now, I frequently evaluate both my performance and market behavior to ensure that my objectives stay achievable and relevant.

Using Goal Setting to Build Confidence

Achieving small, reasonable targets on a consistent basis can boost a trader's confidence significantly. When you achieve a target, you build trust in your process and reinforce the discipline required to thrive in day trading. This confidence can also help you overcome losing streaks by reminding you of your previous accomplishments.

When I first set achievable goals, I was shocked by how much confidence I gained. Instead of feeling defeated by little setbacks, I regarded them as part of the route to my next goal. Hitting those little targets kept me focused on my plan and made trading feel more doable and less intimidating.

Setting Goals Beyond Just Profit

Profit is an important component of trading, but ambitions can go beyond financial gain. Setting personal development goals, such as sticking to a strategy, managing emotions better, or enhancing focus, results in a more comprehensive approach to growth. These non-monetary goals contribute to your total achievement by helping you build the mindset and discipline needed for long-term success.

For example, one of my personal objectives was to take breaks after each trade to review my mindset and reset emotionally. This routine helped me avoid making rash decisions and remain grounded, especially after stressful trades. It had a direct impact on my trading success by helping me retain mental clarity and control, even though it was not a profit-related goal.

Accepting Progress Over Perfection

One last facet of goal-setting is valuing progress over perfection. No trader has a perfect record, and focusing only on meeting every profit target can lead to undue stress. Instead, appreciate each modest step forward, knowing that it takes you closer to long-term achievement.

Over time, I learnt to judge my performance based on how much I progressed as a trader rather than meeting every profit target exactly. When I focused on progress rather than perfection, my outlook improved, and I was able to face problems with greater resilience. This mindset has been extremely beneficial in helping me develop consistency, which is the ultimate goal of any day trader.

Final Thoughts on Realistic Goal

Setting

Setting realistic goals is about building a foundation that enables steady, sustainable growth, not about limiting oneself. By striving for attainable, incremental gains, you develop the discipline, confidence, and mental resilience required to succeed in day trading. Profit goals combined with skill development result in a balanced, holistic approach that allows you to traverse market ups and downs without losing focus or momentum.

Remember that trading is a marathon, not a sprint. Setting goals that are appropriate for your level of experience, risk tolerance, and market conditions will pave the way for steady profits and long-term success.

Conclusion

The Path to Understanding Day Trading Psychology

Mastering the mental game of day trading is a difficult journey, but those who are prepared to put in the effort will reap significant dividends. As we have seen throughout this book, the path to regular gains in day trading requires not just technical abilities and methods, but also psychological resilience, emotional awareness, and a commitment to continuous growth. This final chapter brings together the key mental methods we've covered, emphasizing the mindset and tools required for long-term success.

Reflecting on the Power of Psychology in Day Trading.

The importance of psychology in trading cannot be emphasized. While many new traders enter the market with a focus on strategy, those who succeed recognize the need of emotional control, discipline, and mental clarity. Trading psychology has an impact on every decision we make, from whether to enter a trade to when to step away and rest. The ability to retain mental stability in the face of market volatility distinguishes professional, consistent traders from others who struggle.

Consider the importance of emotional discipline, for example. Fear and greed are ubiquitous emotions in trading, and learning to recognize and manage them is critical to retaining control. As previously noted, detecting emotional triggers, developing resilience through practice, and setting realistic goals all contribute to a consistent and methodical approach to trading. This discipline becomes a tremendous anchor, especially on difficult trading days.

Embracing Resilience as a Trader's Most Important Asset

In day trading, a robust mindset is crucial. Losses are unavoidable, and even the most seasoned traders face losses. What matters is not avoiding losses, but learning how to deal with them productively. Resilience allows us to recover from losses without having an impact on our confidence or motivation. This skill enables traders to retain a good attitude even during difficult times, reinforcing the assumption that setbacks are transient.

When I think back on my own journey, I remember the days when a streak of losses would bring frustration and self-doubt. It required time and a commitment to personal growth to develop the resilience to view losses as learning opportunities rather than failures. I progressively changed my trading strategy by cultivating a resilient mindset, embracing the notion that every trade, profitable or not, contributed to my long-term success. This mindset is not only necessary for dealing with losses, but also for being grounded during periods of success, which is also critical for maintaining consistency.

Developing Focus, Self-control, and Discipline.

Day trading requires the ability to focus and retain self-control in a high-stress setting. The market moves swiftly, and diversions can result in costly blunders. Learning to focus on the work at hand, block out unnecessary information, and stick to a predetermined plan are all important skills that may be improved with practice and self-awareness.

Another factor that has a significant impact on trading success is impulse control. Impulsive acts, such as pursuing a trade or straying from your strategy due to impatience, can result in big losses. By establishing the discipline to stick to a well-thought-out plan, traders can reduce the impact of emotions and make more informed judgements.

A significant turning point in my trading career occurred when I began using tactics to improve my focus. I developed a routine that included pre-trading activities such as evaluating my strategy and reflecting on previous deals. This habit enabled me to enter each trading session with a clear mind and a set strategy, eliminating the possibility of impulsive behavior. My trading strategy was revolutionized by a focus on self-control and discipline, allowing me to execute deals with increased confidence and precision.

Using Emotional Awareness to Manage Stress

Emotional awareness—recognizing and understanding our emotions—is a skill that considerably helps us deal with the pressures of trading. Traders who can recognize their emotions are better able to make decisions uninfluenced by fear, greed, or frustration. Traders can effectively handle and manage their emotions if they acknowledge them rather than suppress them.

Stress management is also crucial for maintaining a balanced trading attitude. High-stress conditions can impair judgement, making it difficult to think properly and make wise decisions. Traders can manage their stress levels using techniques like mindfulness, deep breathing, and breaks. Incorporating these activities into one's daily routine can greatly improve emotional regulation and general well-being.

On a personal level, adopting mindfulness techniques helped me keep cool and collected, even on days when trades did not go as expected. Learning to halt, breathe, and reset my mental state significantly improved my ability to approach each trade rationally, free of the emotional baggage of past deals. This practice became a cornerstone of my trading psychology, and I strongly recommend it to any trader looking for consistency.

Setting Realistic Expectations and Goals for Sustainable Growth.

Realistic goal planning is an essential component of long-term trading success. Many traders enter the market with high hopes, only to be disappointed when they fail to accomplish their goals. Setting modest, attainable goals allows traders to focus on long-term improvement rather than quick success, which is more sustainable and less emotionally exhausting.

Small, attainable goals act as milestones, instilling confidence and motivation. For example, focusing for consistent weekly gains rather than doubling your account in a short amount of time will help you develop a more sustainable trading strategy. Setting realistic goals helps traders manage their expectations, reduce emotional stress, and develop a growth mindset.

When I began focusing on incremental targets, my trading became significantly more stable. Each modest success boosted my confidence and helped me stick to my strategy. Over time, I realized that the journey of day trading is about consistent development rather than rapid returns. This adjustment in viewpoint helped me become a more disciplined and patient trader, and I hope it inspires others as they pursue their own trading ambitions.

Staying committed to continuous learning and improvement.

The market is continuously changing, and traders must be prepared to adapt and change alongside it. Continuous learning—whether through trade evaluation, market trend analysis, or strategy refinement—is critical for long-term success. Keeping a trading log, reflecting on each trading session, and learning from other traders are all beneficial activities for growth and adaptability.

One of the most satisfying features of day trading is that the journey is never completely over. Every day brings new insights, difficulties, and opportunity for improvement. Embracing a continuous learning mindset helps traders remain resilient and adaptive, which are crucial attributes in a continuously changing market.

Final Thoughts on Understanding Day Trading Psychology

The journey to mastering day trading psychology is not short or easy. It is a process of personal development, self-awareness, and commitment. Each of the elements we've addressed, from emotional discipline and resilience to goal-setting and continual learning, is essential for developing a trading mindset that promotes persistent success.

Finally, mastering day trading psychology yields not only financial gains, but also personal transformation. The abilities you develop as a trader—discipline, resilience, patience, and adaptability—go beyond the trading floor and have a favorable impact on other areas of life.

Day trading evolves into a journey of self-discovery, a test of character, and a path to personal strength.

Remember that every trade, success, and setback contributes to your improvement as you continue on your trading journey. By cultivating a resilient and disciplined mindset, setting reasonable goals, and being devoted to continual improvement, you may navigate the market with confidence and attain the consistency that distinguishes successful traders.

Stay focused, grounded, and open to the process. The journey to mastering day trading psychology is about becoming the best version of yourself, one trade at a time.

GET INSTANT ACCESS TO THE FREE VIDEO COURSE BY CLICKING OR COPYING AND PASTING THE LINK BELOW TO YOUR BROWSER!!

https://mailchi.mp/8465a286d83d/chinedu-brown-fx

Happy Watching!!